# A Clandestine Operation

A Play by Phil Mansell

SILVERMOON
PUBLISHING
www.silvermonpublishing.co.uk

# SILVERMOON
## P U B L I S H I N G

A Division of Silvermoon Productions Limited
3rd Floor I 207 Regent Street I London I W1B 3HH
0207 096 0979
www.silvermoonpublishing.co.uk

ISBN 978-1-910457-22-1

Silvermoon Publishing is an innovative publishing house established to publish plays and license rights to theatre companies world-wide. Silvermoon aims to promote its plays and playwrights to ensure that its playwrights get maximum exposure.

*For Terry, the "Colonel" aka Torbay's Man of Mystery.*

# PHIL MANSELL

Phil Mansell originally trained at the London Film School where he specialised in script-writing, directing and animation, and had three films screened at the National Film Theatre. After teaching film-making, photography and art, he moved into the world of advertising and PR. He was a professional writer until he took early retirement from his job as Press and Communications Officer at the University of Wales, Newport where he also gained an MA in Multimedia and Information Design.

Phil has had four other plays published by Silvermoon. His full length play According to Claudia was selected by Newport Playgoers Society to launch their 92nd season and won the Award for Theatre Show of the Year 2014 presented by entertainment and lifestyle magazine Voice.

Poor Yorick was a winning entry in a competition run as part of the Royal Shakespeare Company's Open Stages project and was performed at both the 400-seat Dolman Theatre and Blackwood Little Theatre. Bunkered was a winning entry in a golf-themed play-writing competition, judged by celebrated Welsh playwright Frank Vickery, to celebrate the Ryder Cup being held in Newport. The play enjoyed a week long run at the Dolman Theatre. Caddying for Godot was short-listed in the same competition.

He has also won the drama section of the annual writing competition organised by the University of Wales, Newport and judged by Wales's national poet, Gillian Clarke, who wrote of Phil's work: "The dialogue is completely convincing, funny and touching."

Phil has also had five books published in the Netherlands and Denmark, three books for teenagers and two books, which he also illustrated, for younger children.

# Characters

Bray            an operative

Crowe           an operative

Adler           their female superior

Dawn            a knife-thrower's assistant


Bray and Crowe are very different. Crowe is supercilious and has a very superior attitude. He is smartly dressed in neatly ironed shirt and tie. Bray is somewhat ineffectual, untidy and wears a cardigan over a crumpled shirt open at the neck. He is quite clearly bored by his work.

Their superior, Adler, is smartly dressed and very officious.

Dawn is a young and attractive innocent abroad. She wears a skimpy, sequinned showgirl top and has long fishnet clad legs.

The setting is a bare shadowy room with a door, a small table and two chairs. On the table is a large hourglass, a soup spoon and a plate on which is a lump of cheese and some bread. There is a large old-fashioned telephone on the floor with a line going off. There is an open doorway out of the room leading to other rooms, including a pantry. The effect should be film noir meets steam punk.

**Music:** Sad, haunting cello solo.

*BRAY sits on a chair by the keyhole of the door, whistling to himself. From outside comes the sound of someone hand-cranking a car followed by a man testing a microphone, saying "1...2...3...testing" and reciting 'Mary had a little lamb'.*

*BRAY looks through the keyhole, tuts, looks around him, sighs and goes back to looking through the keyhole and then sits back. In the distance, from behind the door, is heard the sound of a crowd cheering followed by a fanfare of trumpets. BRAY quickly looks through the keyhole, sighs again and then sits back in his chair, staring at the keyhole. CROWE enters carrying a large bunch of keys. He stands watching BRAY for a few seconds and then jangles the keys noisily to attract his attention.*

**CROWE:** Hello-o!

**BRAY:** Hello.

**CROWE:** I can see you!

**BRAY:** What?

**CROWE:** I can see you.

**BRAY:** What about it? I've never claimed to be invisible.

**CROWE:** Well you should be. Haven't you read the manual?

**BRAY:** Who reads the manual?

**CROWE:** I do, sonny Jim.

**BRAY:** You would.

**CROWE:** The manual states quite clearly the advantages of merging into the background. Making yourself invisible. Didn't you hear me coming?

**BRAY:** Yes, of course I heard you coming. I'm not deaf.

**CROWE:** Then why didn't you scurry away into the shadows and conceal yourself?

**BRAY:** Why should I?

| | |
|---|---|
| **CROWE:** | Because I could have been anybody walking in here, that's why. You didn't know it was me coming in. |
| **BRAY:** | I knew it was you. I recognised the sound of your club foot. |
| **CROWE:** | I haven't got a club foot! |
| **BRAY:** | You have. (*Pause*) Haven't you? |
| **CROWE:** | No. I am plagued with arthritis in my knees, but only an idiot would confuse that with a club foot. |
| **BRAY:** | Are you calling me an idiot? |
| **CROWE:** | This is a serious lapse in security. I may well have to report it. |
| **BRAY:** | Oh, get stuffed. |
| **CROWE:** | You're lucky I wasn't her ladyship. Has she shown her face at all while I've been gone? |
| **BRAY:** | No. God knows where she's got to. |
| **CROWE:** | Probably powdering her nose. She should never have been put in charge of this operation. |
| **BRAY:** | Because she's a woman? |
| **CROWE:** | I've got nothing against women. They're all well and good in their place. |
| **BRAY:** | Which is where, exactly? |
| **CROWE:** | Ah, you don't catch me out like that. I'm not having you label me as a chauvinistic misogynist. |
| **BRAY:** | You are though, aren't you? |
| **CROWE:** | Of course I am. It's the only way to get on in this game. |
| **BRAY:** | Unbelievable. |

*CROWE picks up the telephone from the floor.*

CROWE:          All lines of communication still down, I take it.

BRAY:           As far as I know. Nobody's called us anyway. Not even
                double glazing salesmen. In fact, I'm so bored I would
                actually welcome a call from a double glazing salesman.

CROWE:          (*Into phone*) Hello? Hello! Anybody there! Dead as a
                dodo. (*He puts the phone back on the floor*) Waste of
                bloody time having it here. How are we supposed to report
                in - by pigeon post?

BRAY:           Can't do that. No pigeons left. You strangled the last one.

CROWE:          It was asking for it. It was bloody noisy, that bird.

BRAY:           Bit harsh, though. Strangulation.

*CROWE goes over to the table and picks up some cheese and eats it.*

CROWE:          So. No sign of Madam Adler. All quiet on the western
                front, then.

BRAY:           Yes. It's been as quiet as the proverbial since you killed
                the pigeons.

CROWE:          Too bloody quiet. You have been listening?

BRAY:           Listening and watching, as instructed.

CROWE:          But nothing's happened? Nothing at all.

BRAY:           Not a sausage.

*There is the sound of cannon firing a salute in the distance. Neither of
them react.*

CROWE:          Have you been at this cheese?

BRAY:           What?

CROWE:          There's a huge chunk of this cheese gone missing.

BRAY:           I haven't touched the cheese. I'm fed up to the back teeth
                with cheese.

CROWE:      Well, there's a chunk gone missing.

BRAY:       Are you accusing me of taking it?

CROWE:      All I'm saying is, there's a big chunk of cheese gone missing.

BRAY:       I've been too busy with this keyhole to eat cheese. It's a full-time job this is.

*CROWE sniffs the cheese and nibbles a bit off. Pause.*

CROWE:      So, what's the situation out there?

BRAY:       Search me.

CROWE:      They should be getting ready about now. Can't you see them getting ready?

*There is another distant sound of cannon firing a salute.*

CROWE:      What was that?

BRAY:       I don't know.

CROWE:      Look through the keyhole – that's what it's there for.

*BRAY peers through the keyhole.*

BRAY:       I can't see a bloody thing. (*He gives up looking through the keyhole*)

CROWE:      It sounded like cannon firing.

BRAY:       Cannon? It was thunder. Cannon!

CROWE:      Sounded like cannon to me. A twenty-one gun salute, if I'm not mistaken.

BRAY:       Twenty one gun salute! It was a clap of thunder. Why would they be firing a twenty-one gun salute, for crying out loud?

CROWE:      I don't know. Look through the keyhole and see.

*BRAY peers through the keyhole.*

**BRAY:**          I can't see a thing...

**CROWE:**      You should be able to see something, if it's only people putting up bunting and floral decorations.

**BRAY:**          I told you I can't see anything.

**CROWE:**      You can't see any bunting?

**BRAY:**          No bunting, nothing.

**CROWE:**      You are looking through the keyhole, aren't you?

**BRAY:**          Of course I'm looking through the keyhole. You think I don't know how to use a keyhole?

**CROWE:**      Well, what can you see?

**BRAY:**          I told you, bugger all.

**CROWE:**      You must be able to see something. I could see plenty of things when I was looking through it earlier.

**BRAY:**          Well, I can't see anything now.

**CROWE:**      You can't see anything? Have you broken it?

**BRAY:**          What do you mean, broken it? You can't break a keyhole!

**CROWE:**      Well it was working perfectly all right when I looked through it. I could see all sorts of things clear as a bell. There was a man carrying a tray of pastries. I could see him quite clearly. He was carrying a silver tray full of pastries. On his head.

**BRAY:**          On his head?

**CROWE:**      The tray was balanced on his head.

**BRAY:**          Were they Danish pastries?

**CROWE:**      I don't know. They were on a tray. On his head.

**BRAY:** I'm quite partial to Danish pastries. I could just go a bit of Danish pastry right now. Be better than that mouldy cheese.

**CROWE:** Have another look.

**BRAY:** I told you, I can't see anything. I think somebody's put something in the way.

**CROWE:** They can't put things in front of that door. It's against health and safety, surely.

**BRAY:** Be that as it may, somebody has definitely plonked something down on the other side.

**CROWE:** You mean there's something obscuring the view?

**BRAY:** That's right. There's something been plonked down.

**CROWE:** What is it?

**BRAY:** I don't know. Could be anything. A large earthenware pot. Or maybe an old fashioned gramophone.

**CROWE:** Well make your mind up. There's a world of difference between an earthenware pot and an old fashioned gramophone.

**BRAY:** I can't make out what it is.

**CROWE:** You might as well say that your view is being obscured by the great pyramid of Giza.

**BRAY:** It might well be for all I can tell.

**CROWE:** That's highly unlikely though isn't it. Given where we are and what's about to occur.

**BRAY:** All I know is, I can't see anything. Maybe somebody's put it there to stop us seeing what's happening.

**CROWE:** No... They don't know we're here. Do they? You don't think they know we're here?

**BRAY:** I don't know. Do you think they know?

**CROWE:**   I bloody hope not. Someone'll be for the high jump if they know we're here.

*ADLER enters, looking around furtively. BRAY fails to notice ADLER but CROWE ducks back into the shadows. ADLER goes straight to the hour glass on the table.*

**ADLER:**   How long has this hourglass been like this?

**BRAY:**   I didn't see you come in.

**CROWE:**   (*Emerging from the shadows*) I did. I spotted you. That's why I hid.

**ADLER:**   I'll say it again. How long has this hourglass been like this?

**BRAY:**   Like what?

**CROWE:**   I heard you coming and I slipped into the shadows. You could have been anybody. So I....

**ADLER:**   The sand's all gone through. Look. Look here.

**CROWE:**   You could have been anybody. But I was ready.

**ADLER:**   You were supposed to turn it over when all the sand had gone through. Didn't you notice all the sand had gone through?

**BRAY:**   I was too busy here. I'm on keyhole duty. I thought Crowe was looking after it.

**CROWE:**   Me? I thought you were keeping an eye on it.

**ADLER:**   We were using this to time the entire operation.

**BRAY:**   I can't look through here and watch that thing.

**ADLER:**   Now we don't know where we are. The timing will all be out.

**CROWE:**   We could synchronise watches. Would that help?

**ADLER:**   We aren't using watches. We're using this.

| | |
|---|---|
| **BRAY:** | Don't worry, we've got ages yet. |
| **ADLER:** | For your information we have not got ages. We've got an hour at the most. Right, I'm going to turn it over now. (*She turns the hourglass over*) When all the sand's run out we should be through that door and on our way. |
| **BRAY:** | An hour? How do you reckon we've only got an hour? |

*ADLER picks up the phone.*

| | |
|---|---|
| **ADLER:** | Any luck with the phone? |
| **CROWE:** | Still out of commission. |
| **ADLER:** | (*Into phone*) Hello. Hello? Custard Cream calling Chocolate Hobnob. Are you receiving me, Hobnob? Come in, Hobnob. |
| **CROWE:** | Custard Cream and Chocolate Hobnob! Who was the bright spark who thought up those code names? |
| **ADLER:** | It was me, actually. |
| **CROWE:** | Inspired. Absolutely inspired. Fond of biscuits are you? |
| **ADLER:** | (*Replacing the phone on the floor*) It's dead. Either the line's been cut or they've all gone home. |
| **BRAY:** | Maybe they're out there, enjoying the festivities. |
| **ADLER:** | That's highly un- Listen....Hear that? |
| **BRAY:** | What? |
| **ADLER:** | Listen.... |

*They listen. In the distance can be heard the sound of a barrel organ.*

| | |
|---|---|
| **BRAY:** | What is it? |
| **ADLER:** | The hurdy-gurdy's started up. They'll be firing the cannon soon. As soon as they start firing the cannon our time's up. Now, keep an eye on that hourglass. Both of you. Or do I have to do everything myself? Idiots. |

*ADLER exits smartly. CROWE looks after her and smiles smugly.*

**CROWE:**     She really fancies me, you know.

**BRAY:**      Cannon?

**CROWE:**     What?

**BRAY:**      She said once they'd fired the cannon...

**CROWE:**     I told you it was cannon. A twenty-one gun salute.

**BRAY:**      That was never twenty one guns. Twelve maybe...

**CROWE:**     A minute ago you thought it was thunder. I take it you've
               had no luck with the lock?

**BRAY:**      Well I'd hardly be looking through the keyhole if I'd
               managed to unlock the door would I?

**CROWE:**     No luck with the lock then?

**BRAY:**      No. No luck with the lock at all. Those keys we were given
               are bloody useless.

**CROWE:**     They're standard issue keys.

**BRAY:**      That explains it.Bloody useless.

**CROWE:**     Well, try these then.

*CROWE hands BRAY the big bunch of keys.*

**BRAY:**      Where'd you get these?

**CROWE:**     I found them in the pantry.

**BRAY:**      What were you doing in the pantry?

**CROWE:**     I was having a mooch around. I was hoping to find some
               pickled onions to go with the bread and cheese, and there
               they were - hanging on a nail.

**BRAY:**      Any luck with the pickled onions?

CROWE:        No pickled onions. No red cabbage. Nothing.

BRAY:         Pity. I'm quite partial to pickled onions.

CROWE:        I'm fond of the odd pickled onion too. I could just go a few
              pickled onions now. They'd set this cheese off a treat. But
              all could find were these keys. Hanging on a rusty nail. I
              thought, hello, keys. One of these might open that door.
              So I brought them back here, pronto.

BRAY:         Let's hope you're right. 'Cos the keys we were given are
              bloody useless. I think we're OK now. One of these should
              do the trick, shouldn't it?

*BRAY tries the keys in the lock. CROWE goes to the table and fiddles
with the spoon.*

CROWE:        There was a fanfare of trumpets earlier. Did you hear it?
              Once they've sounded the fanfare of trumpets there's less
              than an hour before the procession starts.

BRAY:         I didn't hear any trumpets. You must be mistaken.

CROWE:        I know a fanfare of trumpets when I hear one.

BRAY:         You must have imagined it.

CROWE:        I am not in the habit of imagining things, especially
              fanfares of trumpets.

BRAY:         Must have been a radio playing somewhere.

CROWE:        There was no radio. The place is deserted. Everyone's
              out there getting ready for the procession.

BRAY:         That's what it was, a radio.

CROWE:        I'm not going to be preached at by someone who can't
              see through a keyhole.

BRAY:         I'm not preaching. And I can see through keyholes.

*CROWE sits down and starts picking at the cheese.*

CROWE:        Are you sure you haven't been at this cheese?

**BRAY:** No! I told you. I've been too busy.

**CROWE:** Well, someone's been at it. There's dirty great lumps been taken out of it.

*There is a distant fanfare of trumpets.*

**BRAY:** Hear that?

**CROWE:** What?

**BRAY:** That fanfare.

**CROWE:** What fanfare?

**BRAY:** That fanfare of bloody trumpets that just sounded!

**CROWE:** Is that what it was? I thought it was elephants.

**BRAY:** That means things will be livening up soon. Better get this bloody door open.

**CROWE:** Sounded like a herd of elephants at a distant watering hole to me.

**BRAY:** What are you talking about, distant watering hole? It was definitely trumpets.

**CROWE:** Elephants trumpet, don't they.

**BRAY:** Oh, elephants trumpet, admittedly. I'll give you that. They don't do bloody fanfares, though, do they.

**CROWE:** I bet they could with a bit of expert training. It's amazing what you can train elephants to do. There was a man in Bognor Regis, he trained an elephant to fetch his newspaper from the shop every day.

**BRAY:** It was trumpets.

**CROWE:** Or it might have been Bombay. Yes. More likely to have been Bombay than Bognor if elephants were involved.

**BRAY:** None of these bloody keys fit. I've forgotten which ones I've tried now. I'm going round in circles here.

CROWE: What we need is someone who can pick a lock. If only Jenkins was here.

BRAY: Orlando Jenkins? The ex-sheep-farmer?

CROWE: A dab hand at picking locks. Absolute disaster as a human being, but a dab hand at picking locks.

BRAY: I didn't know that. I thought his speciality was blowpipes.

CROWE: Oh he's very good with blowpipes. When it comes to utilising a blowpipe, Jenkins is a bloody genius. But it's a little known fact that he can also turn his hand to picking locks.

BRAY: I've always wondered about blowpipes... Those tribes that use blowpipes, they put poison on them, don't they?

CROWE: Yes. They smear the tips of the darts with very potent home-made poison. Kills instantly.

BRAY: That's what's got me confused. If they were to go hunting in the jungle and shoot, say, a monkey up a tree with a blowpipe, how is it safe to eat if the dart's covered in this terrible poison?

CROWE: I don't know. All I know is the monkey's dead before it hits the ground.

BRAY: I don't think Jenkins uses poisoned darts.

CROWE: Put it this way, he doesn't use them to knock monkeys out of trees. No. He has other fish to fry.

BRAY: I heard he uses lives eels.

CROWE: Live eels? Where did you hear that?

BRAY: It's rumoured that he shoots live eels through his blowpipe.

CROWE: Whatever for?

BRAY: I don't know. It's just something he does. A sort of party turn.

CROWE:     Oh yes. I can just see that breaking the ice at some posh cocktail party.

BRAY:      I didn't say he does it at cocktail parties. Just...ordinary parties.

CROWE:     What, birthday parties? Are you saying he's a children's entertainer? Is that another string he's added to his bow? You'll be telling me he makes balloon animals next.

BRAY:      He may well do for all I know. Talented chap, Jenkins. He can turn his hand to most anything.

*There is the sound of approaching footsteps.*

CROWE:     Someone coming! Quick!

*They both hurry to a dark corner and hide. ADLER enters.*

ADLER:     Isn't that door open yet?

*They come out of hiding.*

CROWE:     We're nearly there.

ADLER:     The procession will be over by the time we get it open.

CROWE:     We're working as hard as we can.

ADLER:     What are they up to out there? Have the musicians come out yet?

CROWE:     We don't know.

ADLER:     Well, look through the keyhole!

BRAY:      We've tried that but we've hit a snag. There's something in the way.

CROWE:     There's something obscuring the view, apparently. He reckons it's the great pyramid of Giza.

BRAY:      I never said that.

ADLER:     Let me look.

23

**BRAY:** An earthenware pot, I said.

*She pushes BRAY out of the way, kneels down and looks through the keyhole.*

**ADLER:** What are you talking about? I can see everything from here.

**BRAY:** What?

**ADLER:** There's a man in a bowler hat doing tricks with an umbrella and a parking meter. Oh, and there's some majorettes limbering up near the podium.

**BRAY:** What podium? I couldn't see a thing when I looked through there.

**CROWE:** I told you they couldn't have put anything in front of that door. It's against health and safety regulations.

**BRAY:** They might have moved it again.

**ADLER:** And there's the musicians taking the stand.

**CROWE:** How many of those have we got to contend with?

**ADLER:** Four...no, five.

**CROWE:** Not the usual string quartet, then?

**ADLER:** No. Let's see how they line up. There's a harp, a piano accordion, timpani, a flute and a fat woman with a flugelhorn.

**CROWE:** A flugelhorn? Huh! They're pushing the boat out aren't they?

**BRAY:** I couldn't see anything when I looked through there.

**ADLER:** The last of the banners has been put in place.

**CROWE:** What does it say?

**ADLER:** I don't know. It's in Esperanto. (*She stands*)

| | |
|---|---|
| CROWE: | Sounds like they're all set to go, then. |
| BRAY: | I think someone must have put something down temporarily and then moved it again. |
| ADLER: | How soon are you going to have this door open? |
| BRAY: | Well, that depends on how soon we can find a key that fits the lock. |
| ADLER: | Don't any of those fit? |
| BRAY: | No. |
| ADLER: | Bloody useless! Where did you get them from? |
| BRAY: | He found them. In the pantry. |
| ADLER: | What were you doing in the pantry? Your orders were to stay here and get this door open before the procession starts. |
| BRAY: | He was looking for some pickled onions. |
| ADLER: | What? You left your post to go looking for pickled onions! |
| BRAY: | Or some red cabbage. |
| CROWE: | I thought it might liven up this bread and cheese a bit. It's as dull as ditchwater eating this twenty four hours a day. |
| ADLER: | So you just strolled off in search of assorted condiments. |
| CROWE: | I was on the look-out for anything that might help us achieve our objective. That's how I found the keys. |
| ADLER: | And do any of the keys unlock the door? |
| BRAY: | No. They're bloody useless. |
| CROWE: | At least I'm doing something. He can't even look through a keyhole properly. |
| BRAY: | There was something obscuring my view! |

CROWE: She had no trouble seeing through, though did she? It was clear as a bell when she looked through it. Same as it was for me earlier. Seems there's only something obscuring the bloody view when you're peering through it.

ADLER: This is no time to start bickering among ourselves!

BRAY: What are you trying to say? Are you saying that I am unable to carry out a simple procedure like looking through a keyhole?

CROWE: I am saying that you might be visually challenged when it comes to keyholes. That's all.

BRAY: What's that supposed to mean?

CROWE: All right. I'll spell it out for you. The normal procedure when looking through a keyhole is to close one eye. Am I right?

BRAY: That is the standard practice, as laid down in the manual, yes.

ADLER: This is getting us nowhere.

CROWE: Well, I think you're putting the wrong eye up to the keyhole. I think you're putting the closed eye up to it.

BRAY: I'd have to be mad to do that.

CROWE: Well prove it. Look through that keyhole and tell us what you can see.

BRAY: All right. I accept your challenge.

ADLER: This is ridiculous. We should be concentrating on getting this door open.

BRAY: Excuse me. Can I just have a peek?

*BRAY elbows her out of the way and peers through the keyhole.*

BRAY: Aha!

CROWE: See something can you?

**BRAY:** Yes. I can see plenty, thankyou very much. There's some majorettes and some musicians.

**CROWE:** Madam here just told you that. What sort of instruments are they playing?

**BRAY:** There's a harp and a piano and a...er...a glockenspiel.

**CROWE:** Rubbish! You're making it up. You can't see anything through there.

**BRAY:** I can! Hold on. I think the civic dignitaries have just arrived. They're getting out of their vintage limousines. There's the Lord Mayor with his chain of office glinting in the sun. He's getting out of the ceremonial gold coach.

**ADLER:** The Mayor isn't due for another half hour! We're way behind schedule if the Mayor's arrived.

**BRAY:** Oh, maybe it's not the Lord Mayor. It might be a...er... juggler. That's it. It's a juggler.

**CROWE:** You're making it up!

*Sound of instruments tuning up in the distance.*

**ADLER:** Ssshhh! Listen!

*They listen intently.*

**BRAY:** The band's started playing. It's the national anthem.

*He stands smartly to attention.*

**CROWE:** They're tuning up, you twerp.

**ADLER:** We must get this door open! Are you sure you've tried all those keys?

**BRAY:** I think so...

**ADLER:** Give them to me.

*She takes the keys and frantically tries each one in the lock. BRAY leans in close to observe.*

CROWE:      What we need is an expert locksmith. Someone who can pick that lock in the twinkling of an eye.

ADLER:      If only Jenkins was here.

CROWE:      I was just saying that. If only Jenkins was here, I was saying.

BRAY:       He's an expert with the blowpipe and live eel you know.

ADLER:      What?!

BRAY:       Orlando Jenkins. Apparently, he can do amazing things with blowpipes as well as locks.

ADLER:      Will you shut up and get out of my way!

*She shoves him roughly to one side. He strolls over to the table.*

BRAY:       Charming! Looks like someone's starting to panic.

CROWE:      It's a great asset to be calm and collected under pressure. I count myself among the few who are blessed with this rare quality.

BRAY:       Me too. I perform very well under pressure.

            *A louder fanfare of trumpets sounds.*

            Oh God! They're about to start. What are we going to do! We've got to open the door!

CROWE:      All right. Calm down. Pressure getting to you is it?

ADLER:      None of these keys work! This is hopeless! (*She looks through the keyhole*) Oh no! The sergeant at arms is patrolling round the podium.

*The musicians begin to play.*

CROWE:      Sounds like the musicians have started up.

BRAY:       Is it the national anthem?

ADLER:      No. I think it's some ancient Croatian folk song.

**BRAY:**        My favourites.

**ADLER:**        Ssshhh! They're making an announcement.

*An echoey announcement is made through a tinny tannoy system in the distance. The words are mumbo jumbo.*

**BRAY:**        What did he say?

**ADLER:**        Sounded like "The massed ranks of the gold medal bread-makers will now perform the tango".

**CROWE:**        I thought it was "Everyone in the blue seats should make their way to the ornamental fountain".

**ADLER:**        It's starting! They'll be robing up for the procession even as we speak – and we're no nearer getting this door open!

**CROWE:**        Are those keys no good?

**ADLER:**        They're bloody useless! (*She throws the keys onto the floor, stands up and starts pacing round*) This is all your fault!

**CROWE:**        Me? I don't see where I'm to blame.

**ADLER:**        You've had all night to get this door open. What have you been doing all that time?

**CROWE:**        We've tried everything humanly possible.

**BRAY:**        We've been let down by bad keys and shoddy equipment.

**ADLER:**        Well, let me tell you, you haven't heard the last of this. Heads will roll if we don't get through that door in the next five minutes. Do you hear me? Heads will roll!

*She goes towards the other door.*

**CROWE:**        Where are you going?

**ADLER:**        To do what you should have done - get something to open that door.

*She stomps off.*

| | |
|---|---|
| **CROWE:** | She really fancies me. Have you noticed that? |
| **BRAY:** | What? |
| **CROWE:** | She's mad about me. You can tell by the way she looks at me. There's something in her eyes. |
| **BRAY:** | That's rubbish. If she fancies anyone it's me. |
| **CROWE:** | What? She thinks you're a buffoon. |
| **BRAY:** | She does not! |
| **CROWE:** | She thinks you're an idiot. That's as plain as a pikestaff. |
| **BRAY:** | She's a fine one to go calling people idiots. She couldn't get the bloody door open either. |
| **CROWE:** | No, but guess who'll get the blame. |
| **BRAY:** | Who? |
| **CROWE:** | You and me, that's who. |
| **BRAY:** | That's a bit much isn't it? Putting the blame on us. |
| **CROWE:** | It's only too typical of her sort I'm afraid. Women! |
| **BRAY:** | We did our best. |
| **CROWE:** | We can only do what's humanly possible. |
| **BRAY:** | We'll show her. Let's get this bloody door open! |
| **CROWE:** | Good idea. How? |
| **BRAY:** | I'm not sure. |

*Another distant sound effect – church bells toll.*

| | |
|---|---|
| **CROWE:** | Now what's happening? Have a look through the keyhole. |
| **BRAY:** | You have a look. |
| **CROWE:** | You know I can't kneel down, not with my knees. They're like fine porcelain china. |

*BRAY kneels down and peers through the keyhole.*

**CROWE:**    What can you see?

**BRAY:**    Not much.

**CROWE:**    They haven't put another non-existent earthenware pot in the way again have they?

**BRAY:**    No they haven't! Wait a minute – I can see something now.

**CROWE:**    What can you see?

*The sound of horses cantering by.*

**BRAY:**    There's a brass band going by.

**CROWE:**    I can't hear a brass band.

**BRAY:**    They're not playing anything yet.

**CROWE:**    Are they on horseback?

**BRAY:**    They're just marching past, holding their instruments above their heads.

**CROWE:**    Why are they doing that?

**BRAY:**    All part of the ritual I expect.

*Sound of a crowd cheering.*

**BRAY:**    Hello, it's started to rain. It's torrential rain. It's pouring down.

**CROWE:**    Let me see!

**BRAY:**    Everyone's going home. I think they're calling the whole thing off. That's a stroke of luck for us...

*CROWE pulls BRAY aside and with great effort and considerable pain gets down to look through the keyhole.*

**CROWE:**    It's not raining! And there's no bloody brass band...

**BRAY:** They must have gone. They were marching very quickly.

**CROWE:** All I can see is the household cavalry and people milling about, going up to the grandstand to take their seats. Bloody hell!

**BRAY:** What?

**CROWE:** You'll never guess who I can see out there, mingling with the crowds as large as life.

**BRAY:** Who?

**CROWE:** Orlando Jenkins.

**BRAY:** What, the Orlando Jenkins?

**CROWE:** The Orlando bloody Jenkins. As large as life.

**BRAY:** Is he carrying a blowpipe?

**CROWE:** He's got his bag of tricks with him. I dread to think what he's got tucked away in there.

**BRAY:** Live eels, I'll bet.

**CROWE:** Or his lock-picking tools. If only we can attract his attention. He's just the man to get this door open for us.

**BRAY:** Call him!

**CROWE:** Orlando! Hoi, Jenkins! It's no use. The crowd is making too much noise.

**BRAY:** Let me try. (*He gets down to keyhole and shouts through it.*) Orlando! Orlando Jenkins! Over here, Orlando! Mr Jenkins! This way! We need your help! Orlando!

**CROWE:** Any luck?

**BRAY:** I'm flogging a dead duck here.

*He moves away from the keyhole. CROWE looks through once more.*

**CROWE:** It's no good, he's gone. Lost in the crowd.

*There is another incoherent announcement.*

**BRAY:**  What was that all about?

**CROWE:**  I think they're about to start the procession.

**BRAY:**  We're not going to do it, are we? We've failed.

**CROWE:**  Never say die. Where there's a will there's a way. Nil desperandum. (*He stands*)

**BRAY:**  You think we can do it then?

**CROWE:**  Not a bloody chance. Hold on. The phone! (*He picks up the phone and speaks into it.*) Hello! Cream Cracker calling Chocolate Finger. Come in Chocolate Finger.

**BRAY:**  I don't think those are the right code names.

**CROWE:**  Well, they're some sort of biscuit. What else is there?

**BRAY:**  I'm quite fond of coconut macaroons.

**CROWE:**  It definitely wasn't that.

**BRAY:**  Garibaldi? Rich tea?

**CROWE:**  This is hopeless (*Slams down phone*) I need to think. Where's the nearest lavatory?

**BRAY:**  Next to the pantry.

**CROWE:**  Right. Back in a tick.

**BRAY:**  But-

**CROWE:**  It's where I do my thinking. OK?

*He exits. BRAY sits at the table and toys with the cheese. Behind him, the door opens and DAWN enters wearing a skimpy sequinned showgirl outfit and fishnet tights. She looks around then taps BRAY on the shoulder.*

**DAWN:**  Excuse me.

**BRAY:**  (*With a start*) What? Who the devil are you? Where did you come from?

| | |
|---|---|
| **DAWN:** | Are you the knife-thrower? |
| **BRAY:** | What? |
| **DAWN:** | I'm looking for someone to throw knives at me. |
| **BRAY:** | What on earth for? |
| **DAWN:** | Entertainment, of course. That lot out there will lap it up. |
| **BRAY:** | How did you get in here? |
| **DAWN:** | The thing is, we're on in ten minutes and I can't find him. |
| **BRAY:** | Find who? |
| **DAWN:** | The knife-thrower. How many more times? Try and concentrate! Ooh, is that cheese? |
| **BRAY:** | Yes. Do you want some? |
| **DAWN:** | I'd love some. But I'm not allowed. I'm on a strict diet. A knife-thrower's assistant must have a good figure. It's essential. And good legs. Do you think I've got good legs? |
| **BRAY:** | Yes...they're very nice. |
| **DAWN:** | I trained as a dancer. I've won medals. I went to the Sylvia Tafler School of Dance in East Grinstead. You must have heard of it. So, you like my legs? Legs are very important to a dancer. |
| **BRAY:** | I suppose they're more or less essential. Did you just come through that door? |
| **DAWN:** | I can do ballet, tap and jazz. In that order. |

*BRAY goes to the door and tries it but it doesn't open.*

| | |
|---|---|
| **BRAY:** | Odd... |
| **DAWN:** | You should see my pirouettes. Mrs Tafler said they were the finest she'd ever seen, and she's been teaching dance since the year dot. But can I get a job dancing? Can I buggery. Knife-thrower's assistant, that's what I've been reduced to. It's a good job Madam Tafler can't see me now. She'd have a blue fit. She thought I was Royal |

Ballet material. She told me so. "Dawn," she said-

**BRAY:** So you're part of the entertainment. Out there...

**DAWN:** That's right. They blindfold me and tie me spreadeagled to this sort of wooden circle and then spin it round. It goes very fast. I get quite dizzy sometimes. Then there's a roll on the drums and the knife-thrower starts chucking these dirty great knives at me. I can't see a thing. I just hear the thuds. Twelve of them. Thud, thud, thud, thud. One after the other. Above my head, by my sides. He even gets one between my legs. Do you really like my legs? I think they're my best feature. Although some people prefer my boobs. What do you think?

**BRAY:** They're very nice.

**DAWN:** Some people think I've had a boob job. To advance my career, like. I've told them, no chance. I'm not going under the knife. Here, that's funny isn't it? Not going under the knife and me a knife-thrower's assistant.

**BRAY:** Very good. Maybe you should try comedy.

**DAWN:** No, I'll stick to dancing. (*She strikes a few poses*) Got to keep in trim, though. Must look my best. What do you think, about boob jobs?

**BRAY:** I've never really thought about them.

**DAWN:** No? You gay are you?

**BRAY:** No!

**DAWN:** Wouldn't bother me if you was. I'm broad-minded. You have to be in my line of work. I was offered a boob job. Via a friend of mine who's sleeping with a plastic surgeon. I could have had them done wholesale. But I thought no. Real boobs always feel different, don't you think? They're more natural. Here, feel them.

**BRAY:** Pardon?

**DAWN:** Have a feel. See what you think. Real or false? Go on. It's like a taste test.

35

**BRAY:**          No, it's all right. I believe you.

**DAWN:**          Please yourself. The offer was there. (*She looks around*)
                   What you doing here anyway?

**BRAY:**          Nothing. Just observing the proceedings.

**DAWN:**          Oh, an official observer like.

**BRAY:**          Something like that.

*DAWN picks up the hourglass and plays with it, turning it over and over
and watching the sand fall through.*

**DAWN:**          Hey, you don't see many of these about these days, do
                   you?

**BRAY:**          Please don't touch that. It's being used.

**DAWN:**          What for?

**BRAY:**          To time...things.

**DAWN:**          What sort of things?

**BRAY:**          Just things.

**DAWN:**          So you're observing and timing.

**BRAY:**          Yes.

**DAWN:**          But you're not a knife thrower.

**BRAY:**          Afraid not.

**DAWN:**          (*Moving closer to him and flirting a little*) That's a shame. I
                   wouldn't mind you throwing knives at me. You look very...
                   what's the word...trustworthy. I'd feel safe in your hands.
                   Not like some of them others. Drunks some of them. Got
                   the shakes. You don't want someone with the shakes
                   throwing knives at you.

**BRAY:**          I should imagine not.

**DAWN:**          But you, you've got nice steady hands. You could throw
                   knives at me anytime.

**BRAY:**        Thankyou. Very nice of you to say so.

*CROWE enters rubbing his hands frantically.*

**CROWE:**        I give the hand drier in that toilet three out of ten. Pathetic. Be quicker to wave your hands out of the window. If you could open it. Which you can't. (*Seeing DAWN*) Hello. Who's this?

**BRAY:**        This is-

**DAWN:**        Dawn. My name's Dawn.

**CROWE:**        Where did she come from?

**BRAY:**        Out there. She just waltzed in while my back was turned.

**CROWE:**        How did she get in?

**BRAY:**        Through the door.

**CROWE:**        But the door's locked. (*He goes over and tries the door*) It's locked.

**DAWN:**        It opened from the other side no trouble.

**CROWE:**        How much has she seen? What have you told her?

**BRAY:**        Nothing.

**DAWN:**        He said you're observing.

**CROWE:**        You told her that!

**DAWN:**        And timing. Observing and timing.

**BRAY:**        It's no big deal.

**CROWE:**        It is. It's a very big deal. I'm afraid I'm going to have to place you under arrest, young lady.

**BRAY:**        Arrest? That's a bit much, isn't it?

**CROWE:**        I am hereby placing you under close arrest.

| | |
|---|---|
| **DAWN:** | You can't do that. I'm due to have knives thrown at me in five minutes. |
| **CROWE:** | Knives? What knives? |
| **DAWN:** | Bloody big knives. |
| **BRAY:** | She's a knife thrower's assistant. |
| **DAWN:** | Temporarily. I'm a fully qualified dancer in real life. The knife throwing thing is just to tide me over while I wait for a part in a West End show. |
| **CROWE:** | Yes, well- |
| **DAWN:** | I'm auditioning for a musical based on the life of Enid Blyton next week. That looks very promising. I quite fancy the part of Noddy. Or Big Ears, I'm not particular. Can't afford to be, really. |
| **CROWE:** | That's all very well but in the meantime I need to interrogate you. |

*From outside comes another fanfare and a muffled announcement.*

| | |
|---|---|
| **DAWN:** | What was that? Are they announcing the knife throwing? |
| **BRAY:** | I think it was something about acrobats. |
| **DAWN:** | We're on after the acrobats. I've got to go! |
| **CROWE:** | Not so fast. You've got a few questions to answer first. |
| **DAWN:** | What sort of questions? |
| **CROWE:** | I'll ask the questions. |
| **DAWN:** | Yeah, but what sort of questions? |
| **CROWE:** | Come and sit in this chair. |
| **DAWN:** | What for? |
| **CROWE:** | The interrogation. |

| BRAY: | Oh for crying out loud. Just let her go. |
|---|---|
| CROWE: | Sit! |
| DAWN: | I don't want to. You tell him I don't want to. |
| CROWE: | The sooner you sit down, the sooner this will be over. |
| DAWN: | Oh all right then. But I can only stay a couple of minutes. |
| CROWE: | You'll stay as long as it takes. Now. Where's the interrogation lamp? |
| BRAY: | The what? |
| CROWE: | The interrogation lamp. To shine in her face. |
| BRAY: | We haven't got one. |
| CROWE: | Haven't got one? I'll have to use a torch then. Where's the torch? |
| BRAY: | I don't know. |
| DAWN: | Can we get a move on? I've got an appointment with a revolving wooden table. |
| CROWE: | Very well. I can see I'll have to improvise. Now. What's your name? |
| DAWN: | I just told you. Dawn. |
| CROWE: | And who are you working for? |
| DAWN: | I don't know. |
| CROWE: | You don't know? Come along, you can do better than that. I ask you again, who are you working for? |
| DAWN: | And I'll tell you again, I don't know. All I was told was be here at three o'clock and ask for the knife thrower. I don't know his name. |
| CROWE: | And what are you doing in this room? |

| | |
|---|---|
| **DAWN:** | Looking for the knife thrower. Gawd help us... |
| **CROWE:** | What made you think he was in here? |
| **DAWN:** | I don't know. I've looked everywhere else. |
| **BRAY:** | Come on, Crowe. Let her go. She obviously doesn't know anything. |
| **CROWE:** | If this is all too much for you, Bray, I suggest you step outside. Because I tell you, this is going to get a lot tougher and a lot uglier. |
| **DAWN:** | Here, what are you going to do? |
| **BRAY:** | He's not going to do anything. |
| **CROWE:** | Oh yes I am. I'm going to make you talk, young lady. I'm going to make you sing like a canary. When I've finished with you you'll wish you'd never been born. |
| **DAWN:** | I'm not scared of you. I've had knives thrown at me by demented alcoholics. Think I'm frightened of you? |
| **CROWE:** | You will be frightened of me. See this? (*He looks around for something and picks up a spoon from the table*) To you, it's just a dessert spoon- |
| **DAWN:** | It's a soup spoon actually. |
| **CROWE:** | To me it's an implement of torture. I can do things with this spoon that will have you begging for mercy. I have, for want of a better word, my...methods. |
| **BRAY:** | That's it. I'm going to get Adler. She'll put an end to this nonsense. |

*He leaves the room.*

| | |
|---|---|
| **CROWE:** | That's right. You squeamish bastard, you go outside so you don't have to witness what's about to happen. |

*There is a loud roar from the crowd outside.*

| | |
|---|---|
| **DAWN:** | That'll be the end of the acrobats. Look, I've really got to go. (*She makes for the door and tries the handle*) |

| | |
|---|---|
| **CROWE:** | I haven't finished interrogating you yet. |
| **DAWN:** | I can't help that. I've got to get on stage. Can you open the door, please? It seems to be locked. |
| **CROWE:** | I can't open the door. |
| **DAWN:** | No come on, you've had your fun. |
| **CROWE:** | I can't open the door. We've spent half the night trying to open the bloody door. |
| **DAWN:** | Well, it opened for me. |
| **CROWE:** | I think it only opens from the other side. |
| **DAWN:** | You mean it's a one way door? That's ridiculous. |
| **CROWE:** | All I know is we can't open it from this side. Now come and sit down. I've got a few more questions that need answering. |
| **DAWN:** | You're a nutter you are. There must be another way out. Where does that door go? |
| **CROWE:** | Nowhere. Now, sit down or I'll be forced to restrain you. |
| **DAWN:** | Restrain me? What with? |
| **CROWE:** | Rope. |
| **DAWN:** | What rope? |
| **CROWE:** | Just sit down! |
| **DAWN:** | No! I told you, I have to go. |
| **CROWE:** | I'll let you go on one condition. |
| **DAWN:** | What's that? (*He whispers in her ear and makes a clumsy grab at her*) You dirty old man! What do you think I am? |
| **CROWE:** | I know exactly what you are. |

*He grabs her and they struggle. She knees him in the groin and he bends over in agony.*

CROWE:      You stupid bitch! That really hurt.

*ADLER comes back. She is carrying a workman's toolbag.*

ADLER:      Any luck with the door? I've got the very thing here - hello,
            what's going on? (*TO DAWN*) Are you all right? Has he
            hurt you? (*CROWE looks up in amazement still groaning
            and clutching his groin*)

DAWN:       He was going to - he was going to torture me with that
            spoon.

ADLER:      Torture you? With a spoon?

DAWN:       He said he knew ways of using it. He had methods, he
            said.

ADLER:      Take no notice of him. He's a wanker.

CROWE:      Do you mind? She's crippled me!

ADLER:      Stop moaning.

CROWE:      I caught her snooping around. I was going to interrogate
            her.

ADLER:      Why?

CROWE:      To find out what she knows.

ADLER:      Knows about what?

CROWE:      About us. About this...(*Lowers his voice*)...operation.

ADLER:      What's your name, dear?

DAWN:       Dawn.

ADLER:      What do you know about what we're doing here, Dawn?

DAWN:       Nothing.

ADLER:      There you are. She doesn't know anything.

DAWN:       I only came in here hoping to find a knife-thrower.

ADLER:      A knife-thrower? Whatever for?

DAWN:       So that he can throw knives at me.

ADLER:      Of course. You come and sit down here. You must be quite shaken up.

DAWN:       But I've got to get on stage.

ADLER:      What stage?

DAWN:       The stage out there.

CROWE:      I told you. She's come from out there.

ADLER:      Is that right, Dawn? You've come from out there?

DAWN:       I'm part of the entertainment. I've got to get back out there.

ADLER:      But how did you get in?

CROWE:      She came in through the door.

ADLER:      So you've managed to get it open?

CROWE:      No. That's the puzzling thing. It seems you can only open it from the other side.

ADLER:      That's ridiculous. Where's Bray?

CROWE:      He turned squeamish and went looking for you.

DAWN:       I really must go.

*She goes to the door and rattles the handle. The door remains closed. CROWE takes ADLER to one side and talks to her quietly.*

CROWE:      I don't trust her. If you ask me, we should detain her for questioning. She may be able to tell us what's going on out there.

*There is the sound of a huge roar from the crowd outside.*

**DAWN:** I'll tell you what's going on. The knife throwing, that's what's going on. And I'm not there to be thrown at. This is all your fault for keeping me here. That's a hundred quid you owe me.

**CROWE:** A hundred quid?

**DAWN:** It's what I would have been paid. It's the going rate.

**ADLER:** They pay you a hundred pounds to throw knives at you?

**DAWN:** It's highly specialised work. Not everyone can do it.

**CROWE:** Why not? All you do is stand there.

**DAWN:** For your information I don't just stand there. I revolve as well.

*BRAY enters.*

**BRAY:** Did you hear that roar? I think things are kicking off.

**CROWE:** Better check the keyhole then. If you think you can manage it.

**DAWN:** Come on then. Hand it over. A hundred quid.

**CROWE:** You're not getting a penny out of me.

**ADLER:** The important thing now is to get that door open. (*Picks up her toolkit*) I found these in the pantry. There must be something here to help us get the damn door open.

**CROWE:** Well done.

*A huge cheer goes up on the other side of the door.*

**ADLER:** Too late. It sounds like the procession has started. We're not going to make it.

**BRAY:** Here, you'll never guess who we saw out there. Go on, have a guess.

**ADLER:** I don't want to guess.

| | |
|---|---|
| **BRAY:** | Have a guess. It's someone we were talking about earlier. |
| **ADLER:** | I don't know. |
| **BRAY:** | Go on, have a guess. |
| **ADLER:** | I don't want to bloody guess! |
| **BRAY:** | All right, keep your hair on. I'll tell you. It was Jenkins. |
| **ADLER:** | Who? |
| **BRAY:** | Orlando Jenkins. He was out there, walking about as large as life. We tried to attract his attention but it was no use. |
| **DAWN:** | Orlando Jenkins? The ex-sheep farmer? |
| **CROWE:** | You know him? |
| **DAWN:** | Know him? He shot live eels at me once. Through a blowpipe. |
| **CROWE:** | Where was this? |
| **DAWN:** | At a posh cocktail party in Lowestoft. |
| **ADLER:** | Can we focus on the job in hand, please! Our only option now is to watch the whole thing from here. Through the keyhole. |
| **BRAY:** | It won't be the same. |
| **ADLER:** | Of course it won't be the same. We'll have to take it in turns to provide a running commentary. |
| **BRAY:** | Have we got time for that? Look at the hourglass. |
| **ADLER:** | This is no time to start worrying about time. We'll need to compile a full report. Go and get a pen and paper. |
| **BRAY:** | Where from? |
| **CROWE:** | I think I saw some in the pantry. |

**BRAY:**          It's bloody well stocked, this pantry. It's got everything.

**CROWE:**          Not quite. It hasn't got any pickled onions.

*BRAY goes off grumbling.*

**ADLER:**          We're going to have to give a damned good reason why this mission has failed.

**CROWE:**          I don't think we should talk about the mission. Not in front of our sequinned friend here.

**ADLER:**          The powers that be aren't going to be very happy about this. They'll be looking for someone to blame. Heads will roll.

**CROWE:**          They usually do.

**DAWN:**          Here, are you spies or something?

**CROWE:**          Spies? Don't be ridiculous.

**DAWN:**          You are, aren't you? You're spies.

**CROWE:**          You really shouldn't say things like that.

**DAWN:**          What's all this about a mission then?

**CROWE:**          She knows too much. I think I'm going to have to...deal with her.

**ADLER:**          There's no need for that. Come and sit here, like a good girl.

**DAWN:**          I don't like him.

**ADLER:**          Very few people do. Now just sit in this chair and be quiet.

*DAWN sits in the chair.*

**DAWN:**          You are spies, aren't you?

**ADLER:**          Don't be silly. (*She strokes DAWN's face*) Has anyone ever told you you're very attractive?

| | |
|---|---|
| **DAWN:** | Lots of people. |
| **ADLER:** | I'm not surprised. |
| **DAWN:** | I'm a fully qualified dancer. I only do the knife-throwing in between dancing jobs. Mind you, they're few and far between these days. |
| **CROWE:** | I think there's more to her than meets the eye. |
| **ADLER:** | Is that right, my dear? Is there more to you than meets the eye? |
| **DAWN:** | No, not really. With me, what you see is what you get. |
| **ADLER:** | (*Moving closer to her*) What I see is all I'd want. |
| **CROWE:** | Give me five minutes alone with her. I'd make her talk. |
| **ADLER:** | He's a nasty man isn't he? |
| **DAWN:** | I can handle his sort. |
| **ADLER:** | Did you hear that, Crowe? She can handle your sort. |
| **CROWE:** | Five minutes. That's all I'd need. She'd sing like a canary. |
| **ADLER:** | Take no notice, dear. He's all talk. |
| **CROWE:** | I'll show you who's all talk. |

*ADLER takes CROWE aside and they speak in a conspiratorial tone. DAWN leans forward to eavesdrop.*

| | |
|---|---|
| **ADLER:** | Leave the poor girl alone. We have more important things to settle. Like Bray. |
| **CROWE:** | What about him? |
| **ADLER:** | Would you say Bray was to...blame in any way? For the failure of the mission. |
| **CROWE:** | Well, far be it from me to point the finger of suspicion at anyone... |

| | |
|---|---|
| **ADLER:** | Of course, but would you say he's been...an asset on this mission? |
| **CROWE:** | I don't think 'asset' is the word I'd use to describe him, no. |
| **ADLER:** | What word would you use? |
| **CROWE:** | Nincompoop. |
| **ADLER:** | That's an interesting choice of word. In what way has he been a nincompoop? |
| **CROWE:** | Well, I don't like to point the finger but... |
| **ADLER:** | But? |
| **CROWE:** | He has a basic inability to do the simplest tasks. Take looking through a keyhole, for instance. A relatively easy job, wouldn't you say, peering through a keyhole? All one needs is an eye which is placed in close proximity to the keyhole in order to see through it to what lies on the other side. A fairly simple procedure, I would say. Yet Bray seems to be unable to comprehend the logistics of this simple task. He invariably ends up squinting at a close-up of the door. |
| **ADLER:** | And this has affected the success of the mission? |
| **CROWE:** | I should bloody say it has. The mission has revolved around the need to carry out effective surveillance via that keyhole. Whenever Bray's been on keyhole duty I've had the distinct impression his reports have been...how shall I put it? Less than accurate. |
| **ADLER:** | Inaccurate reports, eh? |
| **CROWE:** | In fact, as a result of not being able to see anything through the keyhole, he's been fabricating the whole thing. |
| **ADLER:** | Fabricating? |
| **CROWE:** | Yes, making it all up. Claiming to see a troupe of acrobats dressed as gorillas and the delivery of a giant table-lamp. Added to which he claimed to be an expert locksmith. |

| | |
|---|---|
| **ADLER:** | I thought you were the expert locksmith. |
| **CROWE:** | No. That was Bray. Or so he said. Turns out he can't pick a lock to save his life. From what I've seen of him he has trouble picking his nose. And that's another thing – his personal habits. |
| **ADLER:** | We won't go into that. What you've told me confirms my suspicions. Bray carries a great deal of responsibility for the mission's lack of success. |
| **CROWE:** | Not that I like to point the finger of course. |
| **ADLER:** | Of course. But these things will be duly noted in the report. |
| **CROWE:** | Yes. I think it's important that things are duly noted. Would you like me to mention these things in an official report? Because if you do and it would...help you, then I would want something in return. |
| **ADLER:** | I can't promise you promotion. Not after this fiasco. |
| **CROWE:** | No. I want the girl. |
| **ADLER:** | Which girl? |
| **CROWE:** | (*Nodding at DAWN*) That girl. |
| **DAWN:** | Here, you talking about me? |
| **ADLER:** | Why do you want her? |
| **CROWE:** | I think she knows more than she's letting on. |
| **ADLER:** | You want to interrogate her? |
| **CROWE:** | That's one way of putting it. |
| **ADLER:** | If your version of events were to correspond with mine, I think I can arrange for you to have her. After I've finished with her of course. |
| **CROWE:** | That sounds quite satisfactory all round. |

*CROWE turns and leers at DAWN.*

| | |
|---|---|
| **DAWN:** | Why are you looking at me like that? |

*BRAY returns, carrying some parchment and a quill which he dumps on the table.*

| | |
|---|---|
| **BRAY:** | There you go. This is the best I could find. |
| **DAWN:** | You want to watch it. These two are going to stitch you up. |
| **BRAY:** | What? |
| **CROWE:** | Take no notice of her. I'm going to deal with her later. |
| **BRAY:** | What do you mean, deal with her? |
| **DAWN:** | They're going to put the blame on you. Say it was all your fault. |
| **CROWE:** | I think I'd better silence her. |
| **ADLER:** | There's no need for that. Look...Dawn. You must be quiet. Or I'll have to let Crowe loose on you. And you wouldn't like that. |
| **CROWE:** | No, you wouldn't. |
| **DAWN:** | I'm not frightened of him. |
| **BRAY:** | You really should be. He's rather a nasty character. Do yourself a favour and be quiet. |
| **DAWN:** | I was only trying to warn you. |
| **BRAY:** | Ssshhh. OK? |
| **DAWN:** | Please yourself. It's your funeral. |
| **BRAY:** | Right. Now where were we? |
| **ADLER:** | You were about to start writing the report. |
| **BRAY:** | Me? But I fetched the pen and paper. |
| **ADLER:** | And now you're going to write the report. I shall dictate. |

**BRAY:** Can't he write it? He's hardly done anything on this mission, except sit around eating cheese and scratching himself.

**ADLER:** You seem to have a problem following orders, Bray. I wonder if that is one of the reasons why this mission has been less than successful?

**BRAY:** I've worked bloody hard on this mission. I spent most of the night struggling with that lock. My knees are black and blue.

**ADLER:** Indeed? Then the state of your knees should go in the report. Start writing.

**BRAY:** (*Muttering to himself*) It's always me.

*BRAY sits at the table and picks up the quill.*

**ADLER:** Write the following, in triplicate.

**BRAY:** In triplicate?

**ADLER:** It's an official report.

**BRAY:** That's as may be but in triplicate.... That's nearly twice as much work.

**CROWE:** It's three times as much, actually. Can't do simple maths, either...

**BRAY:** Piss off.

**ADLER:** Right, put the name of the mission at the top.

**BRAY:** What was it called again?

**ADLER:** Operation Clandestine.

*BRAY scratches the quill across the parchment as he writes.*

**DAWN:** Clandestine? What's that mean?

**CROWE:** I'll definitely have to deal with her now. She knows far too much.

ADLER:    The object of the mission – are you writing this down?

BRAY:     Give me a bloody chance.

ADLER:    The object of the mission was to- What was the object of the mission?

CROWE:    To observe and infiltrate the proceedings taking place, as outlined in our written brief.

ADLER:    And how was this to be achieved?

CROWE:    Via that door.

ADLER:    Did you get that, Bray?

BRAY:     Slow down a bit. "Object...of....mission..."

CROWE:    To observe and infiltrate the proceedings taking place, as outlined in our written brief.

BRAY:     Hold on!

ADLER:    And how would you describe the brief?

CROWE:    We had a watching brief. Keeping an eye on things.

ADLER:    Was that all? Just to watch? We also had to infiltrate, surely?

BRAY:     There was a mention of some infiltration.

ADLER:    A mention? Surely the point was to open that door and mingle with the crowds during the proceedings.

BRAY:     We were told to infiltrate if possible.

ADLER:    If possible? And do what?

BRAY:     Mingle.

ADLER:    And mingle. Infiltrate, mingle and note names and faces. That's what we're interested in. Names and faces.

BRAY:     Any particular names and faces?

| | |
|---|---|
| **CROWE:** | Oh, I think we'd know which names and faces. Just by looking at them. Put a name to a face and make a note of it. |
| **ADLER:** | So. How do we rate the success of the mission? |
| **BRAY:** | Ooh, that's a tough one... |
| **ADLER:** | Would you say it's been a success? |
| **BRAY:** | Up to a point. |
| **ADLER:** | Up to what point? |
| **BRAY:** | Well, we did a fair bit of surveillance. |
| **ADLER:** | But no infiltrating? |
| **CROWE:** | No, as it turned out, infiltration was not possible. |
| **BRAY:** | Due to the non-opening of the door, you see. |
| **ADLER:** | And who was to blame for the non-opening of the door? |
| **BRAY:** | Who was to blame? |
| **ADLER:** | Yes, who was to blame for the fact that the door remained locked and unopened? |
| **DAWN:** | You want to watch it. They're going to blame you. |
| **CROWE:** | I've warned you. (*He goes over to DAWN and slaps her across the face*) |
| **BRAY:** | Hey, there's no need for that! |
| **CROWE:** | There's every need. One more word out of you, young lady, and I'm going to take you to...the pantry. |
| **DAWN:** | (*Mocking him*) Oh, not the pantry! Anything but that! |
| **CROWE:** | You may laugh, but there are things in the pantry which will make you wish you'd never been born. |
| **BRAY:** | He's right. There are some dreadful things in that pantry. Best be quiet, eh? |

| | |
|---|---|
| **DAWN:** | I'll be quiet. But don't say I didn't warn you. |
| **ADLER:** | Now where were we? |
| **CROWE:** | Who was to blame for the non-opening of the door? |
| **ADLER:** | Yes. Who do you think was to blame? |
| **CROWE:** | I suppose it depends how you're defining 'blame'... |
| **ADLER:** | Who was responsible for the failure to get the door open? |
| **CROWE:** | I suppose it depends how you're defining 'failure'. |
| **ADLER:** | Let's call it...non-success. |
| **BRAY:** | If you put it like that I suppose there is only one person you could possibly blame. |
| **ADLER:** | Who is that? |
| **BRAY:** | Orlando Jenkins. |
| **ADLER:** | But Jenkins wasn't part of this mission. |
| **BRAY:** | That's right. If he had been we'd have got that door open in a jiffy and been able to carry out loads of infiltrating. |
| **ADLER:** | You can't blame the failure of the mission on a person who was not involved with it. |
| **CROWE:** | He's got a point though. If Jenkins had been assigned to this mission I think we could have counted it as 100% successful. |
| **ADLER:** | I repeat, you cannot blame the failure of the mission on a person who was not involved with it. You might as well blame the failure of the mission on Walt Disney. Or Albert Einstein. |
| **BRAY:** | But they were to blame. They weren't here to ensure its success. If they'd been here who's to know how quickly we'd have got the bloody door open. |
| **CROWE:** | He's got a point. I bet if anyone could have got that door open it was Albert Einstein. He was a bloody genius, you know. |

**BRAY:** I don't think a locked door would have presented him with much difficulty.

**CROWE:** No. He'd have had that door open before you could say e = mc squared.

**ADLER:** It's not good enough.

**BRAY:** Maybe the door was to blame. It was a particularly stubborn door.

**ADLER:** We cannot blame the door.

**BRAY:** God!

**ADLER:** What?

**BRAY:** God was to blame. He wasn't with us on the mission.

**CROWE:** God must have been with us. He's bloody omnipresent.

**BRAY:** You what?

**CROWE:** He's everywhere.

**BRAY:** Well, He wasn't much bloody use was He? That does it – I'm blaming God.

*BRAY starts to write this down.*

**ADLER:** Hold on! You can't blame God. The powers that be won't swallow that.

**CROWE:** Of course they won't. For one thing, half of them question the very existence of God.

**BRAY:** Well, that's their look-out.

**CROWE:** Personally, I lean towards agnosticism. What are your feelings on the subject?

**ADLER:** I feel we need to finish this report, ASAP. We need to put in something with a little more...substance.

**CROWE:** Yes, yes. Quite right.. Something more...substantial. We need to find the right words.

**ADLER:** And the right phrases.

**CROWE:** The right words and phrases are absolutely essential.

**ADLER:** They are of the utmost importance. All of our futures could depend on how we word this report.

*There is a pause as they stop and think. ADLER and CROWE pace up and down. BRAY scratches his head and stares into space.*

**DAWN:** Can I say something?

**CROWE:** No!

**ADLER:** (*Going over to DAWN and leaning in close to her*) What do you want to say, Dawn?

**DAWN:** Couldn't you say that your mission was less than successful due to a combination of factors?

**BRAY:** That's good! We could definitely say that.

**ADLER:** Write it down!

**BRAY:** (*Writing*) The...mission...was un-suc-cess-ful...

**DAWN:** Less than successful...

**BRAY:** Less than suc-cess-ful...be-cause of...

**CROWE:** Due to.

**BRAY:** Due to a num-ber of...

**DAWN:** A combination of.

**BRAY:** A com-bin-ation of...fac-tors.

**CROWE:** A combination of contributory factors.

**BRAY:** Hold on, hold on. Con-trib-u-tory -. How do you spell contributory?

| | |
|---|---|
| **ADLER:** | These comprised circumstances above and beyond the control- |
| **BRAY:** | Hang about! |
| **DAWN:** | Above and beyond the control of the persons responsible for... |
| **ADLER:** | Responsible for? No, no. I don't think it's wise to start attributing responsibility. |
| **CROWE:** | Good point. Big word, responsibility. |
| **DAWN:** | How about - the persons charged with carrying out... |
| **ADLER:** | That's good. |
| **CROWE:** | Charged with carrying out the...the... |
| **DAWN:** | The tasks allotted. |
| **BRAY:** | Slow down! I can't write that fast. |
| **ADLER:** | I like that. The tasks allotted... |
| **BRAY:** | This thing's useless. Has anyone got a ballpoint pen? |
| **DAWN:** | The tasks allotted and defined as part of the brief.... |
| **ADLER:** | Brilliant! |
| **BRAY:** | Or a pencil? |
| **ADLER:** | As part of the brief defined on a need to know basis to those... |
| **DAWN:** | To those who needed to know. |
| **ADLER:** | Very good! Did you get all that? |
| **BRAY:** | No. How am I expected to write with this thing? |
| **CROWE:** | It's a poor workman who blames his tools. |
| **BRAY:** | Piss off. |

| | |
|---|---|
| **ADLER:** | Read it back to me. |
| **BRAY:** | Er, let me see. What have I written here? "The mission was…" What does this say. I can't read my own writing. |
| **ADLER:** | Out of the way! I'll write it. Give it to me. |

*She sits down and starts scribbling with the quill.*

| | |
|---|---|
| **CROWE:** | What are you writing? |
| **ADLER:** | Ssshhh. I'm concentrating. |
| **CROWE:** | Remember what we said. I hope there's no mention of me in that report. |
| **ADLER:** | Don't worry. I shall say that you contributed towards the mission and performed to the full extent of your capabilities. |
| **CROWE:** | Can you make that 'considerable capabilities'? |
| **BRAY:** | What are you writing about me? |

*ADLER ignores this and continues writing.*

| | |
|---|---|
| **DAWN:** | She's writing that you're to blame. |
| **CROWE:** | I'm warning you. The pantry awaits. |
| **BRAY:** | I hope you're mentioning my considerable capabilities. |
| **CROWE:** | And what exactly are your considerable capabilities? Can you name them? |
| **BRAY:** | My capabilities are just as considerable as yours. |
| **CROWE:** | Name one considerable capability that you possess. |
| **BRAY:** | I don't have to justify myself to you. I've done my bit here tonight. |

*There is a distant cheering. BRAY goes back to the keyhole.*

| | |
|---|---|
| **ADLER:** | What was that? What are they up to out there? |

**BRAY:**　　　　They've brought on a matador!

**CROWE:**　　　Let me see.

**BRAY:**　　　　That wasn't in the briefing notes. There was no mention of matadors.

*Engines can be heard revving noisily.*

**CROWE:**　　　What's that? It sounded like motor bikes.

**BRAY:**　　　　It's sheep.

**CROWE:**　　　Sheep?

**BRAY:**　　　　No, I tell a lie. It's a steam engine.

**CROWE:**　　　Let me see!

*He pushes him aside and looks through the keyhole.*

**CROWE:**　　　I can't see a thing. There's something blocking my view.

**BRAY:**　　　　I could see quite clearly.

*The sound of a crowd gasping followed by silence. ADLER joins them at the door. While they are occupied, DAWN reads the report.*

**ADLER:**　　　What was that? What's happened?

**CROWE:**　　　I don't know. I can't see. There's something in the way.

**BRAY:**　　　　Could it be a large earthenware pot, by any chance?

**CROWE:**　　　Possibly. I can't make it out.

**BRAY:**　　　　You might as well say that your view is being obscured by the great pyramid of Giza.

*Distant sound of a gloomy drum roll.*

**CROWE:**　　　Oh no!

**ADLER:**　　　What is it?

CROWE:      I think there's going to be...no, it can't be.

ADLER:      What?

CROWE:      A crucifixion.

ADLER:      That's all we needed.

BRAY:       Let me see.

*He pushes CROWE out of the way and kneels at the keyhole.*

CROWE:      No need to push!

BRAY:       Bloody hell!

ADLER:      We have to get out there! Now!

BRAY:       Oh no...

CROWE:      What's happening?

BRAY:       Don't ask.

CROWE:      I am asking.

BRAY:       Well don't. It's better you don't know...

*The distant roar of a crowd, followed by a brass band and fireworks. DAWN replaces the report on the table and sits down.*

CROWE:      What's going on?

ADLER:      We're too late, that's what's going on. We've failed. Heads will roll, mark my words.

CROWE:      Whose heads?

ADLER:      I'd better file this report.

CROWE:      Whose heads will roll?

ADLER:      Let's just say, certain people who shall remain nameless can expect to hear from central HQ in the morning.

*ADLER picks up the report and goes off.*

**CROWE:**    She can't mean our heads, can she? No. Of course not. She fancies me. You can tell by the way she looks at me. She'd never do that to me...

*BRAY stands up.*

**BRAY:**    I can't watch any more...

**CROWE:**    Is it that bad?

**BRAY:**    No. Someone's put something in the way again. (*BRAY starts picking at the cheese*)

**CROWE:**    What do you think she meant – certain people who shall remain nameless?

**BRAY:**    I don't know. You, probably.

**CROWE:**    There's no way she could have meant me. I've pulled out all the stops on this operation.

**BRAY:**    You didn't crack that lock, though, did you.

**CROWE:**    It wasn't my job to crack the lock.

**BRAY:**    Well, it wasn't mine. I had a watching brief. It's all in the report.

**CROWE:**    She said I had performed to the full extent of my capabilities. My considerable capabilities. No, when she talked about persons who shall remain nameless, she meant you.

**BRAY:**    How could she mean me? I never left my post. I never went sloping off looking for pickled onions and red cabbage.

**CROWE:**    I wasn't sloping off, as you call it. I was reconnoitring.

**BRAY:**    You were AWOL. That's what they'll say at the official enquiry. You left your post.

**CROWE:**    You don't think there'll be an official enquiry?

**BRAY:** Bound to be. She'll see to that. You heard her. Heads will roll.

**CROWE:** Aha! That's right. Heads will roll, she said. Heads plural. That means more than one head.

**BRAY:** I know what plural means.

**CROWE:** It'll be both of us for the chop. Persons who shall remain nameless, she said. Persons, plural. We're both for the high jump.

**BRAY:** I blame that keyhole. It's defective. How are we expected to function efficiently with a defective keyhole?

**CROWE:** The only defective thing round here is your brain. This is all your fault. I was sure she fancied me...

**DAWN:** I know whose heads will roll.

**CROWE:** What?

**DAWN:** I said I know who's for the high jump. I read the report. I read what she wrote while you lot were scrambling around by that keyhole.

**CROWE:** I told you she was working for the other side. Creeping in here, reading top secret official documents. (*He grabs DAWN*) What did it say? Did it mention me?

**DAWN:** Let me go and I'll tell you.

**CROWE:** Not likely. You know far too much.

**DAWN:** I do now. I read the bloody report.

**CROWE:** Tell me what it said!

**DAWN:** Only if you let me go.

**CROWE:** Just tell me.

**BRAY:** What did it say, Dawn? Tell us.

**DAWN:** Let me go! I want to go home.

CROWE:      Very well. You leave us no choice. Tie her up, Bray.

BRAY:       What with?

CROWE:      Use your initiative.

BRAY:       There's only cheese. I can't tie her up with cheese.

CROWE:      Go and look in the pantry. There must be something there.

DAWN:       Don't go! Don't leave me alone with him. He's a nutter.

BRAY:       Don't worry. I'm not leaving this room.

CROWE:      Very well. If Mohammed won't come to the mountain...
            (*He manhandles DAWN towards the door leading to the
            pantry*)

BRAY:       Where are you going?

CROWE:      To the pantry.

DAWN:       Please! Do something.

CROWE:      Tell us what was in the report.

DAWN:       You're hurting my arm!

*BRAY moves to help her but stops when from outside comes the sound of
a bugle playing The Last Post.*

BRAY:       Shushh! What's that? (*He goes to look through the
            keyhole*) Hello. Looks like something's happening.

*While he is looking through the keyhole CROWE forces DAWN to her
knees.*

DAWN:       Please, help me!

BRAY:       They're lowering the flag.

DAWN:       He's hurting me! Do something!

CROWE:      (*Hissing*) Tell me what was in the report. Tell me!

*DAWN gives a gasp, faints and slumps onto the floor. Shocked, CROWE stares down at her in silence.*

**BRAY:**    I can see Adler. How did she get out there? She's got the report! She's handing it to someone. I think it's...yes, it's Jenkins. Orlando Jenkins! You know what this means? Crowe? (*He turns and sees DAWN on the floor*) What's happened? What have you done?

**CROWE:**    Nothing. She fainted, that's all.

**BRAY:**    You're a real bastard, aren't you. I hope you're proud of yourself.

**CROWE:**    Don't be such a fuddy duddy. It was all in the line of duty.

**BRAY:**    Since when was torturing knife throwers' assistants in the line of duty?

**CROWE:**    It was hardly torture. A little bit of rough and tumble. I had far worse in the school playground.

**BRAY:**    You infringed her human rights, you know that.

**CROWE:**    Don't talk to me about human rights. I've had a bellyful of you damned whingers and your human rights.

**BRAY:**    What are you going to do with her?

**CROWE:**    I know what I'd like to do with her.

**BRAY:**    You're an animal, you know that?

**CROWE:**    She's damned attractive, you have to admit that.

**BRAY:**    You disgust me. (*He kneels down beside DAWN*) Come on, wakey wakey. Have we got any smelling salts?

**CROWE:**    Hold that cheese under her nose. That'll do the trick.

**BRAY:**    How are you supposed to treat someone who's fainted? I can't remember.

**CROWE:**    I treat them with contempt.

| | |
|---|---|
| **BRAY:** | Come on now, Dawn. Time to wake up. It's no good. She's not responding. |
| **CROWE:** | Loosen her clothing. Here, let me. |
| **BRAY:** | You keep your filthy hands off her. |

*The sound of a volley of rifle fire echoes outside.*

| | |
|---|---|
| **CROWE:** | Good Lord, what was that? |
| **BRAY:** | (*Dropping DAWN and hurrying to the door*) It sounded like a firing squad. (*He looks through the keyhole.*) It is a firing squad. They're practising. Shooting at two posts against the wall. |
| **CROWE:** | Anyone tied to the posts? |
| **BRAY:** | Not yet... You don't think.... |
| **CROWE:** | What? No! We may have cocked-up the operation a little- |
| **BRAY:** | We cocked-up quite a lot actually. |
| **CROWE:** | Still. They wouldn't put us against a wall and- Would they? |
| **BRAY:** | Depends what  Adler wrote in that bloody report. |

*Another round of rifle fire from outside. A voice is heard barking unintelligible orders.*

| | |
|---|---|
| **CROWE:** | What are they doing now? |
| **BRAY:** | Waiting. Just waiting. (He stands) That's it, then. Finished. All over. |
| **CROWE:** | It's not over till the fat lady sings. |

*From outside comes the sound of a female soprano singing opera.*

| | |
|---|---|
| **BRAY:** | Oh no... |
| **CROWE:** | What is it? What can you see? |
| **BRAY:** | (*Looking through keyhole*) It's a rather obese lady - and guess what she's doing... |

**CROWE:**      Then it's all over bar the shouting.

*Sounds of crowd shouting.*

**BRAY:**      I think it's over. (*He stands*)

**CROWE:**      Better go then. Get it over with.

*They exit towards the pantry. There is a short pause. The phone begins to ring. DAWN stands up, dusts herself off, picks up the phone and answers it.*

**DAWN:**      Hello. Dawn to Dusk. Dawn to Dusk. Come in, Dusk. Yes. It's all gone according to plan....No, they've just left... Thankyou, Dusk. Oh, if you insist, Mr Jenkins... Thankyou, Orlando...Yes, I'll rendezvous with you as arranged. Oh, and Orlando - don't forget the knives.

*She replaces the phone, looks around quickly, takes a small piece of cheese to chew then goes to the door. She bangs twice and turns the handle. The door opens. She goes out, closing the door behind her.*

*From behind the door comes the sound of 'Land of Hope and Glory'.*

*Lights fade to black.*

**CURTAIN**

## ALSO BY PHIL MANSELL

# ACCORDING TO CLAUDIA
(4f, 3m) Drama - Full Length

This play is about the secrets that emerge when a family gathers to celebrate the 80th birthday of a crusty Oxford don. His daughters add fuel to the fire by bringing along partners who include a confused crime writer and a former gangster returning from the Costa del Crime. Mix in a dotty maiden aunt, a sad spinster and a mystery gunman and it adds up to a birthday party none of them will forget.

"Insightful, touching, heart-warming and at times hilarious. Compelling viewing."
*The South Wales Argus*


# POOR YORICK
(2f, 3m) Comedy - One Act

Yorick the jester is not dead – he's on the road dying a death as he pioneers a new kind of comedy called stand-up. When this fails, he is persuaded by his tavern wench girlfriend Bess to return to Elsinore and get his old job back – but when he arrives he finds there have been many changes, and he becomes embroiled in Hamlet's plans for revenge.

Winner of the No Holds Bard Festival of One Act Plays run as part of the Royal Shakespeare Company's Open Stages project.


# BUNKERED
(2f, 3m) Comedy - One Act

Business is bad at Tom's run-down crazy golf course and the Igloo Ice Cream Parlour where his friend Kath works. All the holidaymakers are going to the spanking new pleasure beach at the other end of the bay. All looks lost until ageing hippy dropout and sandwich board man Dylan comes to the rescue.

# OTHER PLAYS PUBLISHED BY SILVERMOON PUBLISHING

**Flushed**
by Ron Nicol
(3f)
It's a singles night, and Jan and Meg are taking a break in the Ladies Room. Jan is criticising Tara, unaware that Tara is hiding in one of the toilet cubicles. When Tara's presence is revealed a fight ensues and Jan confesses the reason for her jealousy. Then Meg discovers that the door to the room seems to be locked, and the succeeding series of mishaps and misfortunes ruins Jan's appearance and assurance. Tara eventually manages to open the door, but on the threshold of escape they find that Meg is trapped in one of the cubicles.

**The Beginner's Guide To Murdering Your Husband**
*or (Ten Easy Steps To Becoming A Widow)*
Unwisely written by David Muncaster
(3f,2m)
This play is presented as though it is an instructional video that the audience are watching being filmed. Maddy will present a variety of methods for disposing of an unwanted husband, aided by Jim, her real life husband, and her faithful employees. But is she really trying to get rid of her husband? Is the video just a ruse to lull him into a false sense of security? The parallels with their real life relationship give Jim plenty to worry about but, as the play reaches its its climax, we realise that nothing is what it seems. Criss-cross indeed!

**The World and its Arse**
by David Muncaster
(6m,6f)
Frank's mind plays tricks on him as horrors from his past torment him. Len has nothing but memories. Brian doesn't know what he's got. He probably shouldn't even be there but he has nowhere else to go. A few days in an NHS ward give us a glimpse into the lives of a diverse set of people.

You see all sorts in here
Any colour, any class, any religion
Disease doesn't discriminate
You get the world and its arse come through that door

**I Gave You My Heart**
by David Muncaster
(2f)
Kate has received a parcel through the post from her ex-boyfriend. Her sister, Jenny thinks it is sweet, sending her a nice little parting gift. But Dan isn't sweet according to Kate. He's a freak, a weirdo. And whatever is in that box is somehow related to the last thing that he wrote on Kate's Facebook page – "I gave you my heart"

**Nativity**
by Jonathan Hall
(2m, 3f)
It's December 1979 and class 2G are getting ready for the school Nativity. Gemma wants to be Mary but because she's got a big loud voice she's the narrator, and anyway Sarah her best friend is far loads prettier than her, everyone says so. And as for Kirsty- she doesn't even get a look in, not that she cares, she's bothered about showing her knickers in the practical area. And of course there can only be one choice for Joseph, and that'd have to be Tony, everyone's favourite, complete with his thirteen colour biro. And Nicholas? In love with Sarah and dreams of flying through the milky way with her in the TARDIS? He's always going to be the Innkeeper.

Nativity is about the play we've all been in. About tea towels on heads and coconut-shell donkey hooves. Dinner ladies and toilet roll angels, reading books and Blue Peter. It's about our six year old selves, the adults that shaped us, the dreams that lit our days- and the people we have become.

**Agatha Crusty And The Murder Mystery Dinner**
by Derek Webb
(5m,6f)
Geoffrey and Caroline Robertson are having a dinner party to celebrate ten successful years of Mighty Midget Vacuum Cleaners, the company he jointly owns with Tim McArthur, and to add spice to the evening they decide to make it a murder mystery dinner. They are joined by a variety of employees and their partners. And Geoffrey has a special surprise – he has invited the well-known crime novelist Agatha Crusty (pronounced Croosty) to join them. She is in the area promoting her latest book and agrees to be guest of honour.

But on the evening of the dinner, their remote Victorian house finds itself in the centre of a storm so bad that the river floods and they are cut off. Worse, the power fails and in the darkness one of the guests is murdered. But since everybody else was together when the murder was committed, they are as perplexed as they are worried. And when another murder happens in the same way it is no laughing matter... except this is an Agatha Crusty murder mystery so there are laughs a-plenty. And also a genuine mystery that will keep an audience guessing as well as laughing.

# The only monthly magazine passionate about amateur theatre

amateurstage
PASSIONATE ABOUT AMATEUR THEATRE
www.asmagazine.co.uk
OCTOBER 2013
NEWS | TRAINING | COMMENT | NATIONAL DIARY | INTERVIEWS

going up
MUSIC THEATRE SOUTH
LIFT

IN THIS ISSUE
> Loserville is released
> Making press releases work
> Put the fun into fundraising
> Playscript reviews

amateurstage
PASSIONATE ABOUT AMATEUR THEATRE
www.asmagazine.co.uk
NOVEMBER 2013
£2.95
NEWS | TRAINING | COMMENT | NATIONAL DIARY | INTERVIEWS

nice work...
Chelmsford AODS
Crazy For You

IN THIS ISSUE
> Ticket sales - it's in the detail
> Interview with Philip Meeks
> Win a production - Royalty FREE!
> Playscript reviews

www.ingramcontent.com/pod-product-compliance
Lightning Source LLC
Chambersburg PA
CBHW071635040426
42452CB00009B/1631